The Love Songs of Vidyāpati

Harsha V. Dehejia
Krishan Lal Sharma

Art Consultant
Vijay Sharma

DK PRINTWORLD
Publishers of Indian Traditions

Cataloging in Publication Data–DK
[Courtesy: D.K. Agencies (P) Ltd. <docinfo@dkagencies.com>]

The love songs of Vidyāpati / [text by] Harsha V. Dehejia,
Krishan Lal Sharma ; art consultant, Vijay Sharma.
p. cm.
English and Hindi.
ISBN 9788124607282

1. Vidyāpati Ṭhākura, active 15th century — Criticism and interpretation. 2. Vidyāpati Ṭhākura, active 15th century — Illustrations. 3. Love poetry — History and criticism. 4. Maithili poetry — History and criticism. 5. Rādhā (Hindu deity) in literature. 6. Krishna (Hindu deity) in literature. 7. Rādhā (Hindu deity) — Art. 8. Krishna (Hindu deity) — Art. 9. Painting, Indic. I. Dehejia, Harsha V. II. Sharma, Krishan Lal.

DDC 891.4541209 23

ISBN 978-81-246-0728-2
First published in India in 2014

Printed and published by:
D.K. Printworld (P) Ltd.
Regd. Office : *'Vedasri',* F-395, Sudarshan Park
New Delhi – 110 015
Phones : (011) 2545 3975, 2546 6019
Fax : (011) 2546 5926
e-mail : indology@dkprintworld.com
Web : www.dkprintworld.com

The Love Songs of Vidyāpati

Vidyāpati (c. 1352–1448), called second Jayadeva in his lifetime, is immersed, charged and inspired by the love of Rādhā and Kr̥ṣṇa. He wrote emotionally-intensive love songs in Maithili, for the queens of Śiva Siṁha, his patron, and the common folk. Though drawn inspiration from Jayadeva, more than him, Vidyāpati presents in his poetry a rare, tender and sensitive understanding of Rādhā's psyche. In his love songs Rādhā, not Kr̥ṣṇa, is in the centre stage and through his *nāyikā* Vidyāpati is reaching out to each and every woman in Mithila.

Vidyāpati presents his songs from a woman's heart, and describes his *nāyikā*'s slowly awakening youth, her sensuous beauty, her coyish charm, her naïve innocence, her surrender to love and her anguish on being neglected. She is invariably sensual, spiritual, physical and emotional. Though she did not inspire painters of the time, she ruled the hearts of the people of Mithilā. Vidyāpati's love songs are written in honeyed words and are sung with mellifluous notes in homes, fields, *chowk*s and *havelī*s, across eastern India. And thus he still rules their heart.

This portfolio, based on the ten love songs of Vidyāpati, presents lovely paintings on the varied love moods of Rādhā, the love queen. In doing so, different artists have displayed their dexterity in Jaipur, Caurapañcāśika, late Mughal, Manaku, Kishangaṛh, Jain, Kāngṛā and Basohli styles.

The Author

Harsha V. Dehejia has a double doctorate, one in medicine and other in ancient Indian culture, both from Mumbai University. He is also a member of the Royal College of Physicians of London, Glasgow and Canada all by examination. He is a practising Physician and Professor of Indian Studies at Carleton University in Ottawa, Canada. His main interest is in Indian aesthetics. He has published more than twenty research publications, curated many exhibitions and made a documentary film, *Ateliers of Love, 500 Years of Krishna Paintings.*

The Love Songs of Vidyāpati

The ancient kingdom of Mithilā, located in present-day north Bihar, has a hoary past. *Śatapatha Brāhmaṇa* makes the earliest mention of the colonization of this area by the Aryans. Mithilā was the first region to be Aryanized but the culture of Mithilā shows a combination of Aryan and non-Aryan elements. Initially it was called Videha after its king Videgha. Later a ruler named Mithi founded the city of Mithilā as the capital of the kingdom. Thus Videha began to be called Mithilā. At the time of the Mahābhārata war, Mithilā was a powerful kingdom and there is some evidence that the Pāṇḍavas had occupied this territory. However Mithilā was most celebrated city in *Rāmāyaṇa* as the birth place of Sītā. Buddha stayed in the *vihāra*s of Mithilā and so did Mahāvīra. In the third century BCE Aśoka from his capital in Pāṭaliputra unified the entire country and that put an end to Mithilā's independence and it was then ruled by the southern kingdom of Magadha. Mithilā however never lost its unique cultural character and has been the land of poets and artists, thinkers and philosophers. Vālmīki is believed to have lived here and so did Kālidāsa, and by the eleventh century Mithilā dominated eastern India in cultural matters. Closer to our times it was Vidyāpati who with his sweet love songs in Maithili brought Mithilā once again to our attention. Stretching from the right bank of Gaṅgā to the foothills of the Himalayas Mithilā was an idyllic place with red and yellow blossoms, verdant groves and orchards of mangoes and bananas, and it is because of this feature Mithilā is also called Madhuban.

Vidyāpati (*c.* 1352–1448) was called the second Jayadeva even in his lifetime for he was charged and inspired by the love of Rādhā and Kr̥ṣṇa. He was responsible for bringing glory to this ancient kingdom in medieval India through his love songs. He was a court-poet of Śiva Siṁha, son of Deva Siṁha, and he was greatly attached to his patron. Śiva Siṁha had many wives and one of the reasons why Vidyāpati wrote love poems was to entertain them. A story is told when Śiva Siṁha was summoned by a Muslim king to answer a charge, Vidyāpati went with his patron as an escort and when Śiva Siṁha was brought before the king Vidyāpati pleaded for his release by offering to display his psychic powers. The king locked Vidyāpati in a box and sent a group of courtesans of the court to bathe in the river. Vidyāpati was asked to describe what had happened at which time he recited one of his verses describing a woman at her bath. The king was pleased, he pardoned Śiva Siṁha and the two returned to Mithilā and Śiva Siṁha gifted the village of Bisapī to Vidyāpati. Vidyāpati was ever grateful for this gift and in many of his songs he would sing the glory of Śiva Siṁha and his queens. Vidyāpati departed from the norm of writing in Sanskrit, which was the court language, and chose to write in Maithili instead. This was an important departure even though he was versatile in Sanskrit grammar and literature. One reason for this could be that in the neighbouring kingdom of Gauṛ or Bengal the Muslim rulers of the fourteenth century had popularized the use of Bengali and this may have influenced Śiva Siṁha to encourage Vidyāpati to write in the native Maithili. A more probable reason is that Vidyāpati, in keeping with the tradition of Buddha and Mahāvīra who were also natives of Mithilā, wanted his songs to reach the queens of the kingdom and common people of Mithilā and therefore moved away from Sanskrit. Vidyāpati not only made poetry accessible to the ladies of the court but took poetry to the streets and the people of Mithilā. Vidyāpati's Maithili had a certain sweetness and fragrant earthiness that endeared it to the common people of Mithilā and spoke to them with a disarming directness.

While Vidyāpati is credited with many texts he is remembered and valorized most for his love songs. Vidyāpati was probably not a Vaiṣṇava, as there is some evidence that he might have been a Śaivite in his personal beliefs. But 200 years before him Jayadeva had immortalized Rādhā and Kr̥ṣṇa as the romantic couple and all of India was humming with the songs of *Gīta Govinda*. Vaiṣṇavism was acquiring a new resurgence and *śr̥ṅgāra bhakti* a new outlet. Touched and inspired by this Vidyāpati also wrote love songs based on the beautiful love of Rādhā and Kr̥ṣṇa, and continued the ethos of *śr̥ṅgāra* in the context of Vaiṣṇavism. While *Gīta Govinda* was a poetic drama, Vidyāpati wrote individual songs which presented romantic moments rather than a narrative and mostly centred on the love of Rādhā and Kr̥ṣṇa.

Vidyāpati, more than Jayadeva, presented in his poetry a rare, tender and sensitive understanding of Rādhā's psyche. While Jayadeva was a Kr̥ṣṇa-*bhakta*, Vidyāpati was probably not and he upheld Rādhā as a perfect *nāyikā* and through her he reached out to every woman of Mithilā. While describing the *nāyikā*'s slowly awakening youth, her sensuous beauty, her coyish charm or her naïve innocence, her surrender to love and her anguish when neglected, Vidyāpati presents it from a woman's point of view. Vidyāpati truly had a woman's heart and the beauty of his *nāyikā* is not only sensual but spiritual, not just physical but equally emotional, and while his poetry did not inspire painters it ruled the hearts of the people of Mithilā. It is still a common practice in rural Bihar to ask a newly-wed bride how many Vaidyāpati songs she knows.

Mithilā in the time of Vidyāpati was influenced also by the cult of Tantra. With its emphasis on woman as *śakti* it is more than likely that this played a part in shaping Vidyāpati's aesthetic sensibility. Fertility, fecundity, agriculture and sensuality were a part of this and it was to colour the culture of Mithilā. Vidyāpati's representations of *śṛṅgāra rasa* of Rādhā and Kṛṣṇa admit erotic images, which are above and beyond romantic moments, and this probably comes from his Tāntric leanings. Vidyāpati's romantic lyrics are earthy, not courtly, and in his world birds and *sakhī*s intermingle with the loves and laments of the lovers. In his poetry the parrot and the cuckoo are a part of the lovers' world. Vidyāpati sings of a fragrant world shared by bees and where love is carried not just by words but by the dust of pollen.

Vidyāpati describes spring nights of longing that are made up of flowers in groves, humming bees and trumpeting elephants, moonlight and sandal paste and a bed of *kunda* flowers. For him, Rādhā has the fragrance and delicacy of *mālatī* flower as is very clear when he says that the forest has burst open with white *kunda* blooms but the bee is enraptured by *mālatī* and her honey. Vidyāpati captures the excitement of spring for Rādhā with these words: Blue lotuses flower everywhere and black *kokila*s sing.

Vidyāpati encapsulates the beauty of the romantic moment of *virahiṇī* Rādhā in these words: The moon spits fire, lotuses droop, *kokila* bird of spring why do you sing your love-provoking song? For Vidyāpati, there is a correspondence between the mind of *nāyikā* and the landscape of Mithilā, for one evokes the other, one is a reflection of the other and, thus, when the wind blows through the trees of Mithilā even today they seem to whisper one of Vidyāpati's heart-throbbing songs. Vidyāpati may have had a Śaiva ancestry but his inspiration and refuge was always Hari. He writes: *darśan lagi punae nita kām, anukhan japae to hari pae nām*. He founded no sect and laid down no dogmatic creed but his world-view was shaped by the love of Rādhā and Kṛṣṇa. To be a witness to the eternal love of Rādhā and Kṛṣṇa was his constant longing, *duhu jan akul duhu karu kor, duhu darsane vidyāpati bhor*. He bases his compositions on the Kṛṣṇa of *Bhāgavata* and Rādhā of *Gīta Govinda,* but departing from both presents a unique picture of their love. For instance, when Kṛṣṇa goes to Mathurā Vidyāpati has a messenger take Rādhā's message to him and he goes counter to tradition and has Kṛṣṇa return to Vṛndāvana.

Maithili had close affinity with Bengali, Odiya and Assamese, and it is because of this that Vidyāpati is considered a poet of those regions as well. Caitanya was strongly influenced by Vidyāpati and so was Shankardeva of Assam and Vidyāpati's *pada*s are an important part of eastern Vaiṣṇavism. Vidyāpati took the art of composing *padāvalī*s to a new height and these were to become the precursor of later Vaiṣṇava *padāvalī*s and *bhajanāvalī*s. Rabindranath Tagore, writing about Vidyāpati, states, "His poems and songs were one of the earliest delights that stirred my youthful imagination". Vidyāpati remains unrivalled as a poet of love who not only had a vivid imagination but equally a quickened heart that was responsive to love in all its manifestations. Poetry for him was not mere literature but a way of life. His poetry was written with honeyed words and was sung with mellifluous notes in homes and fields, *chowk*s and *havelī*s all over eastern India. In his own words: *madhur madhur ras gān, madhur vidyāpati bhān,* mellifluous are his songs and sweet is Vidyāpati.

Harsha V. Dehejia

महाकवि विद्यापति

विद्यापति का जन्म स्थान मिथिला प्रदेश के दरभंगा ज़िले के अंतर्गत "बिसपी" गाँव माना गया है। यह गाँव राजा शिवसिंह ने विद्यापति की विद्वत्ता का सम्मान करते हुए तथा उनकी कविताओं से प्रसन्न होकर उन्हें दान कर दिया था। शिवसिंह के राज्यारोहण का वर्ष ई. सन् 1411 माना गया है। अतः गाँव के दानस्वरूप प्राप्त होने का काल भी यही, या, इसके आसपास माना जाना चाहिए। विद्यापति मैथिल ब्राह्मण थे और इनके कुल की उपाधि ठाकुर थी। इनके पूर्वजों में अनेक विद्वान् हुए और वे दरबार में उच्च पदों पर आसीन भी थे। स्वयं विद्यापति के पिता पं. गणपति ठाकुर भी राजमंत्री थे और उन्होंने *रागभक्तितरंगिणी* की रचना की थी। यह सचमुच खेद का विषय है कि इतने महान् कवि की जन्म व मृत्यु की तिथियों के सम्बन्ध में कोई प्रामाणिक उल्लेख नहीं मिलता है और न ही विद्वानों में इस पर कोई सर्वसहमति बन पाई है। अतः इस विषय में हम थोड़े से उन निष्कर्षों तक ही स्वयं को सीमित रखना चाहेंगे जो डॉ. शिवप्रसाद सिंह जैसे विद्वानों ने गहन अध्ययन के पश्चात् निकाले हैं। *कीर्तिलता* कवि की प्रथम रचना है जिसमें विषय को क्रमबद्ध विस्तार दिया गया है। इसका काल-निर्धारण हो जाने से उसके जन्म वर्ष का भी कुछ अनुमान लगाया जा सकता है। राजा गणेश्वर की मृत्यु ई. सन् 1372 में हुई और *तारीख़-ए-मुबारकशाही* के अनुसार सुल्तान इब्राहीम शाह जौनपुर की गद्दी पर ई. सन् 1401 में बैठा। अतः कहा जा सकता है कि राजा कीर्तिसिंह अपने पिता के हत्यारे असलान को दंड देने के लिए अपने भाई वीरसिंह के साथ सुल्तान के पास सहायता माँगने के लिए ई. सन् 1402 में गए होंगे। उनके साथ विद्यापति भी थे। राजा कीर्तिसिंह के राज्यारोहण के साथ ही विद्यापति की राजकवि के पद पर नियुक्ति हुई होगी और तभी उन्होंने इस घटना को स्मरणीय बनाने के लिए *कीर्तिलता* की रचना की होगी। इस तर्क के सहारे विद्यापति का जन्म 1374 ई. के आसपास ठहरता है।

अब कवि के निर्वाण समय को लें। एक पद में उन्होंने लिखा है कि राजा शिवसिंह के युद्ध-क्षेत्र में तिरोधान के बत्तीस वर्ष बाद उन्होंने एक स्वप्न देखा और उन्हें अपनी मृत्यु का आभास होने लगा। राजा शिवसिंह का तिरोधान 1415 ई. माना जाता है। इस आधार पर कवि का निर्वाण वर्ष 1447 ई. ठहरता है, या, इसे दो-तीन वर्ष कुछ और आगे बढ़ाएं तो ई. सन् 1450 मान सकते हैं। इसी तरह उनकी जन्म-तिथि को भी कतिपय विद्वान् कुछ और पहले खिसकाने के पक्ष में हैं। अस्तु। राज्य-प्राप्ति के कुछ वर्ष बाद ही कीर्तिसिंह की मृत्यु हो गई। उनके बाद थोड़े समय के लिए पहले भवसिंह फिर देवसिंह गद्दी पर बैठे। देवसिंह के अत्यंत वृद्ध होने के कारण उनके जीवनकाल में ही उनके पुत्र शिवसिंह राज-काज संभालने लग गए थे, उनका विधिवत् राजतिलक 1411 ई. में हुआ। शिवसिंह और विद्यापति बाल-सखा थे इसलिए उनका राज्यकाल कवि के जीवन का भी सुख-समृद्धि की दृष्टि से श्रेष्ठतम काल रहा। उनके रचित अनेक पद शिवसिंह और उनकी पत्नी लखिमा देवी की प्रेम-क्रीड़ाओं को समर्पित हैं। लखिमा देवी अत्यन्त सुंदर थीं और कवयित्री तथा काव्य-मर्मज्ञ भी थीं। कहा जाता है कि अंतःपुर में विद्यापति के गीतों का राजा-रानी के समक्ष सस्वर पाठ होता था। कुछ गीत तो यह आभास देते हैं मानों कवि स्वयं अपने आश्रयदाता के सामने पाठ कर रहा हो। ये गीत ही उनकी अक्षय कीर्ति के आधार हैं। भारत के सभी प्रदेशों में तीज-त्यौहार, उत्सव-विवाह तथा उपनयन आदि संस्कारों के अवसरों पर स्त्रियों द्वारा गीत गाए जाने की प्रथा है। मिथिला जनपद के अन्तर्गत इन गीतों में विद्यापति द्वारा बनाए गए पदों की संख्या सर्वाधिक रहती है जिससे अनुमान लगाया जा सकता है कि आज भी जनता के हृदय पर उनका अधिकार है। इसका मूल कारण है इन पदों में प्रयुक्त वह जनभाषा जो सीधे लोक-हृदय को प्रभावित करती है। इन पदों में विद्यापति मुख्यतः रति भाव के कवि रहे हैं। श्रृंगार रस के सभी पक्षों को उन्होंने जीवन की विभिन्न परिस्थितियों के परिप्रेक्ष्य में देखा है और ऐसा करते समय उनकी दृष्टि प्रधानतः राधा-कृष्ण/नायक-नायिका के अतुलित सौंदर्य पर रही है क्योंकि वे ही रस परिपाक के आलंबन विभाव हैं। इस कोण से विचार करने पर वे "सुंदरम्" के कवि ठहरते हैं और कभी तो ऐसा प्रतीत होता है मानों उन्हें तो बस राधा-कृष्ण के अलौकिक सौंदर्य का ही वर्णन करना है। श्रृंगार के विविध पक्ष तो केवल निमित्त हैं। उन्होंने इसे "अपरूप" (अपूर्व) कहा है क्योंकि यह गोचर होते हुए भी अनुभूति में अलौकिक है। अलौकिकता का प्रथम गुण है उसका विराट् होना। अपरूप ऐसा धर्म नहीं है जो केवल देह तक सीमित होकर रह जाए। यह अपनी व्यापकता में संपूर्ण धरती और आकाश को समेट लेता है। कृष्ण का रूप ऐसा ही है –

कमल जुगल पर चाँदक माला, ता पर उपजल तरुन तमाला।
ता पर बेढ़लि बीजुरी-लता, कालिंदी तट धीरे चलि जाता।

दोनों पांवों के नाखूनों की शोभा ऐसी है जैसे अनेक चंद्रमाओं की एक माला बन गई हो। शरीर पर धारण किया हुआ पीतांबर ऐसा है मानों बिजली ही लता बनकर देह से लिपट गई हो। चंद्रमा और बिजली का कृष्ण का देह-धर्म बन जाना उनका अवरोहण नहीं है वरन् विराट् ब्रह्म के संयोग से उनके सौंदर्य का आरोहण है, लौकिक से अलौकिक हो जाना है। राधा के संदर्भ में यह भाव और भी स्पष्ट है –

देख-देख राधा रूप अपार।
अपरुब के बिहि आनि मेराओल खिति-तल लावनि सार।

राधा का रूप अपार है, उसका केवल संकेत ही दिया जा सकता है और कवि ने वही किया है। उसके अनुसार यह समस्त संसार के लावण्य का सार है जिसे ब्रह्मा ने राधा के रूप में रच दिया है। फिर इस रूप की शक्ति देखिए –

जहाँ-जहाँ नयन विकास, तहिं-तहिं कमल परकास।
जहाँ लहु हास संचार, तहिं-तहिं अमिय बिथार।

वे जिधर देखती हैं उसी ओर कमल ही कमल खिल उठते हैं। कमल यहाँ सौंदर्य का पुंजीभूत रूप है। तात्पर्य यह कि संसार का समस्त सौंदर्य राधा की दृष्टि से ही जन्म लेता है। इसी तरह उनकी मंद मुस्कान से चारों ओर अमृत ही अमृत बहने लग जाता है। यह है उनका विराट् रूप।

"अपरूप" की दूसरी विशेषता है "तिल-तिल" नूतन होना। इसमें क्षण-प्रति-क्षण ऐसा परिवर्तन होता रहता है कि सौंदर्य और निखरता जाता है। यह भी उसके अपार्थित होने का एक प्रमाण है –

सखि, कि पूछसि अनुभव मोय।
सेहो पिरित अनुराग बखानिये, तिल-तिल नूतन होय।

यह प्रीति और अनुराग जन्म-जन्मांतरों का है फिर भी वह नित नवीन होता जाता है, क्योंकि वह रूप ही ऐसा है जिसमें तिल-तिल (क्षण-प्रति-क्षण) नूतनता जन्म लेती रहती है और, यह नित्य नया बना रहने वाला रूप अलौकिक ही हो सकता है। "अपरूप" की नित नूतनता की प्रत्यक्ष अनुभूति कवि ने राधा की वयःसंधि के वर्णन में स्वयं भी की

है और सहृदय को भी कराई है। शरीर के एक ही अंग को लेकर केवल दो पंक्तियों में उसने राधा को शैशवावस्था से निकालकर यौवनाधिरूढ़ा बना दिया है –

पहिलें बदरि कुच पुन नवरंग, दिन-दिन बाढ़ए पिड़ए अनंग।
से पुन भए गेल बीजकपोर, अब कुच बाढ़ल सिरिफल जोर।

उरोजों की अंतःगति से उनमें होने वाले परिवर्तन से उत्पन्न सौंदर्य की उसने जिस बिंबात्मक भाषा में अनुभूति कराई है वह हिंदी साहित्य में बेजोड़ है। उरोज पहले बेर के जितने बड़े हुए, फिर देखते-देखते नारंगी के आकार के हो गए। दिन-प्रति-दिन, अब कामदेव उसे अधिक पीड़ा देने लगा है। फिर, न जाने कब, उरोज बिजौरा (बड़ा) नींबू के आकार के हो गए और अब कुच बेल-फल के जोड़े के रूप में बढ़ने लगे हैं। इन पंक्तियों को पढ़ते-पढ़ते मन वयःसंधि के रूप-लावण्य में डूबता जाता है।

जहाँ तक प्रेम के विविध पक्षों के निर्वाह का प्रश्न है वह परंपरागत है। दूती का दोनों पक्षों को मिलने के लिए प्रेरित करना, नोक-झोंक, फिर मिलन और विरह उसी प्रकार से वर्णित हैं जिस तरह से पहले भी वर्णित किए जाते रहे थे। इन वर्णनों में जो मुख्य है वह है कवि की निजता-प्रेम की व्याकुलता, अनुभूति की तीव्रता और रचना-कौशल जो संयोग और वियोग दोनों ही पक्षों में अत्यन्त भावावेग पूर्ण बन पड़ा है। विरहिणी का यह दुःख,

सखि, हमर दुखक नहिं ओर।
ई भर बादर माह भादर, सून मंदिर मोर।

भला किसे करुणा-विगलित नहीं कर देगा। प्रतीत होता है राजा शिवसिंह के तिरोधान के पश्चात् रानी लखिमा देवी के दुःख ने कवि को झकझोर दिया था, वही आवेग उसके विरह-प्रसंगों में फूट पड़ा है।

अंत में दो शब्द कवि की समाजोन्मुखी दृष्टि पर। हमारी दृष्टि में विद्यापति एक जागरूक कवि थे, समाज को उन्होंने खुली आँखों से उसके समग्र रूप में देखा था। हम यहाँ दो उदाहरण और प्रस्तुत करना चाहते हैं। अनमेल विवाह उन दिनों कोई अघट घटना नहीं थी। कवि ने ऐसी ही एक पीड़िता के दुःख को देखा और समझा, तब इस पर जो व्यंग्य प्रहार उन्होंने किया वह अनोखा है। किसी परिस्थितिवश एक युवती का विवाह बालक से हो गया। कल्पना कीजिए कि बालक पति को लेकर उसका कितना अपमानजनक उपहास होता होगा। दूसरे, उसका निजी जीवन भी कितना विडम्बनापूर्ण हो गया होगा। अंत में उसका आक्रोश इन पंक्तियों में फूट पड़ता है –

हमरी समाद नैहरे ले ले जाउ।
कहुहिन बाबा के किनए धेनु गाइ।
दुधवा पियाइ के पोसता जमाइ।।

वह अपने नैहर (पिता के घर) संदेश भिजवाती है कि अपने [दूधमुँहे] जमाई के दूध पीने के लिए गाय भिजवा दो। इस मार्मिक व्यंग्य में छिपी पीड़ा से सहृदय कहीं गहरे आहत हुए बिना नहीं रह सकता। ऐसी ही करुणापूर्ण पंक्तियाँ एक कूटनी-वेश्या के संदर्भ में भी आई हैं। वह अपना यौवन कुत्सित प्रेम-व्यापार में बिता चुकी है, अब वृद्धावस्था में कभी अपनी उस भूल को स्मरण कर आँसू बहा लेती है तो कभी वर्तमान में होने वाली दुर्दशा से कराह उठती है –

कय परमाद धिया मोर भेल . . .

उसे सबसे अधिक पीड़ा इस बात की है उसके चरित्र के कारण उसकी बेटी को न जाने कितने तिरस्कारपूर्ण प्रवादों का सामना करना पड़ रहा है। फिर उसे स्वयं भी तो जब न तब अपमानजनक स्थितियों को झेलना पड़ता है –

खने खस घोघट विघट समाज, खने-खने अब हकारिल लाज।

दुष्ट समाज के बीच उसका घूँघट जिस क्षण खिसक जाता है, या खिसका दिया जाता है (वृद्धावस्था में घूँघट उसके लिए अपनी कुरूपता को छिपाने का साधन है) तो वह क्षण-क्षण में लज्जा को पुकारती है। समाज उसे घृणा की दृष्टि से देखता है, किंतु कवि ने उसका चित्रण सहानुभूतिपूर्वक किया है। वह पश्चात्ताप की अग्नि में जल रही है किंतु कवि की दृष्टि में समाज भी उतना ही दोषी है बल्कि उसका दोष व्यक्ति के दोष से कहीं अधिक है। ऐसी प्रवृत्तियों को प्रश्रय देने के कारण सबसे बड़ा अपराधी तो वही है। सारांश यह है कि समाज में व्याप्त विसंगतियों, कुरीतियों को उजागर कर कवि ने अपने सामाजिक उत्तरदायित्व का निर्वाह किया है। अतः कहा जा सकता है कि उसके सामने समाज की आशाओं, आकांक्षाओं को अभिव्यक्ति देना, या उसका मनोरंजन करना ही प्रयोजन नहीं था, उसे शिक्षा देना, उसका मार्गदर्शन करना वह अपना धर्म समझता था। इस तथ्य को स्वीकार कर लेने पर हम देखेंगे कि विद्यापति को सच्चे अर्थ में युग-धर्म का निर्वाह करने वाला युग-कवि कहना सर्वथा उचित होगा।

डॉ. कृष्ण लाल शर्मा

1. The Lonesome Lover

The flower has blossomed in the midst of thorns
hence, the distressed bee cannot approach it.
The bee has been wandering all over
but it cannot rest until it finds you.
O Mālatī! it looks at you, who is full of honey,
again and again and wants to partake of your honey
even at the cost of its life.
It lives on honey and you are the reservoir of honey.
Don't you feel ashamed to keep all the honey for yourself.
Now, think and come to some conclusion,
if the bee dies, who will get the blame for its death.
Vidyāpati says –
he (the lover) will remain alive only as long as
he is able to partake of the nectar of your lips.

कंटक माझ कुसुम परगास।
भमर बिकल नहिं पाबए पास।
भमरा भेल घुरए सब ठाम।
तोहे बिनु मालति नहिं बिसराम।
रसमति मालति पुन पुन देखि।
पिबए चाह मधु जीब उपेखि।
उ मधुजीबी तोजे मधुरासि।
साँचि धरसि मधु मने न लजासि।
अपनेहु मने गुनि बुझ अबगाहि।
तसु दूषन बध लागत काहि।
भनहि विद्यापति तौं पए जीब।
अधर सुधारस जौं पए पीब।

2. A Bed of Flowers

A bed of flowers
A glowing lamp
And scented sandalwood
Await you.
Whenever you met [her]
Time passed quickly
and she felt the pangs of love.
O Mādhava!
your Rādhā is [today] in the role of *vāsakasajjā*.
Don't delay going to your tryst.

कुसमे रचलि सेजा।
दीपं बहुत तेजा।
परिमल अगर चंदने।
जबे-जबे तुअ मेरा।
निफलें बहलि बेरा।
तबे-तबे पीड़लि मदने।
हे माधव! तोरी राही वासकसज्जा।
गमने न करिअ विलम्बे।

3. Śuklābhisārikā

I am certainly going today, dear friend
and shall not fear the elders at home
I will keep my word
I will apply sandal paste to my skin
I shall deck myself with pearls
my eyes look brilliant without *kājala*
I shall cover my body in a white dress
and walk with leisured steps
even if the sky is lit with thousands of moon
from staring eyes I shall not flinch
nor shall I hide
We conceal only from others.
This (fearlessness) is the source of love.
Vidyāpati says –
young lady courage makes all things work.
This emotion is well understood by Śiva Siṁha,
who remains surrounded by beauties.

सखि हे, आज जायब मोहि।
घर गुरुजन डर न मानब, बचन चूकब नाहिं।
चानन आनि-आनि अंग लेपब, भूषन कए गजमोति।
अँजन बिहुन लोचन-जुगुल, धरत धबल जोति।
धबल बसन तनु झपाएब, गमन करब मंदा।
जइयो सगर गगन ऊगत, सहस-सहस चन्दा।
न हम काहुक डीठि निबारबि, न हम करब ओत।
अधिक चोरी पर सयँ करिअ, एहे सिनेहक सोत।
भन बिद्यापति सुनह जुबती, साहस सकल काज।
बूझ सिबसिंघ इस रस रसमय, सोरम देबि समाज।

4. Mirror

As the mirror to my hand
the flowers to my hair
kājala to my eyes
tāmbūla to my mouth
musk to my breast
necklace to my neck
ecstasy to my flesh
heart to my home
as wings to a bird
water to fish
life to the living
so are you to me.
But tell me
Mādhava, beloved!
who are you?
who are you really?

हाथक दरपन माथक फूल,
नयनक अँजन, मुखक ताम्बूल,
हृदयक मृगमद, गीमक हार
देहक सरबस गेहक सार।
पाखीक पाख, मीनक पानी,
जीवक जीवन हम तुहु जानी,
तुहु कैछे माधव? कहबि मोई।
विद्यापति कहा-दुहु दोहा होई।

5. Master of Love

My Kṛṣṇa is very clever
with no effort on his part
he broke my all resisting pride
today he came garbed as a *yogī*
to mystify me by a trick
ordered by my mother-in-law I went to give him alms
he was overwhelmed at seeing my face
when he begged the jewel of my pride
I knew how cunning was his mind
and then what he said
I am too shy to repeat
no one even knew
that he was the cleverest of all, i.e. the master of love.
Vidyāpati says – O beautiful Rādhā!
surely you could not understand how shrewd he is.

बड़ई चतुर मोर कान।
साधन बिनहि भाँगल मझु मान।
जोगी बेस धरि आओल आज।
के इह समुझब अपरुब काज।
सास बचन हम भीख लइ गेल।
मझु मुख हेरइत गदगद भेल।
कह तब 'मान-रतन दइ मोय'।
समझल तब हम सुकपट सोय।
जे किछु कहल तब कहइत लाज।
कोई न जानल नागर-राज।
विद्यापति कह सुन्दरि राई।
किए तुह समुझबि से चतुराई।

6. Dawn

O Beloved! the night has passed, lotuses are in bloom
the bees are looking out for their mates
light of the lamp has become dim, the sky is red,
all these suggest that it is dawn.
Dearest, please leave me now,
I do not approve of this behaviour
we will meet again, I swear by Kāmadeva
The wise listen to their beloved
So don't be obstinate, dear, it will spoil the joy
While stealing one should stay within limits.
You have tasted nectar, do not detain me.

रयनि समापलि फुलल सरोज।
भमि भमि भमरी भमरा खोज।
दीप मन्द रुचि, अम्बर रात।
जुगुतहि जानलि भए गेल परात।
अंबहुँ तेजहुँ पहु मोहि न सुहाए।
पुनु दरसन होत मदन दोहाए।
नागर राखु नारि मनु रंग।
हठ कएले पहु हो रस भंग।
तत करिअए जत फाबए चोरि।
परजन रस लए न रह अगोरि।

7. Spring

Vṛndāvana bears a fresh look
So are the trees, the blossoms and flowers.
Vasanta has arrived with *malaya* winds,
intoxicated bees *huṁ* and sport
The young Kṛṣṇa, filled with new love, is strolling along
the lush green banks of Yamunā.
Intoxicated by the fresh honey of mango blossoms
the flocks of *kokila*s
are singing and the young damsels are love struck.
It appears, as if new love personified is wandering through
the forest.
Seeing young Kṛṣṇa and beautiful Rādhā dallying in new
ways Vidyāpati is no more in senses.

नब वृन्दावन नब नब तरुगन, नब नब बिकसित फूल।
नबल बसंत नबल मलयानिल, मातल नब अलि कूल।
बिहरइ नबलकिसोर।
कालिंदी पुलिन कुंज बन सोभन, नब नबप्रेम-बिभोर।
नबल रसाल-मुकुल-मधु मातल, नबल कोकिल कुल गाय।
नवयुवती गन चित उमताअई, नब रस कानन धाय।
नब जुबराज नबल बर नागरि, मीलए नब नब भाँति।
निति निति ऐसन नब नब खेलन, विद्यापति मति माति।

8. Time of Love

Tender, beautiful are the new leaves
the forest is wrapped in red
the southern breeze sways
drunken with its scent of blossoms
the spring has arrived in Vṛndāvana and Kṛṣṇa heralds joy
kokila calls from the branch of a mango tree
for the new power reigning the earth
the god of love
the messenger bees after drinking honey
are wandering, watching for women of pride in the forest
Kṛṣṇa, enjoying the beautiful nature,
was busy signalling for the round dance.
The poet Vidyāpati sings the novel emotion of
Rādhā and Mādhava.

अभिनव कोमल सुन्दर पात।
वसन वने जनि पहिरल रात।
मलय-पवन डोलय बहु भाँति।
अपने कुसुम रसें अपने माति।
देखि देखि माधब मन हुलसंत।
बिरिदावन भेल बेकत बसंत।
कोकिल बोलय साहर डार।
मदने पाओल जग नब अधिकार।
पाइक मधुकर कर मधु पान।
भमि-भमि जोहए मानिनि मान।
दिसि दिसि से भमि बिपिन निहारि।
रास बुझाबए मुदित मुरारि।
कवि विद्यापति ई रस गाव।
राधा-माधव अभिनव भाव।

9. Spring, the Season of Love

Trees and creepers have created a pavilion
the clear moonbeams cast a silver light on it
the lotus stem creates a *svastika*
the new leaves have offered him red clothes
O dear lady! get ready to welcome Vasanta
who has arrived in the forest for his marriage
bees sing wedding songs, *koyal*s chant *mantra*s
honey is the sacrament
the moon and the breeze are ready for *barāt*
the golden *palāśa* flowers form a festoon of pearls
the *bela* blossoms are like auspicious rice confetti
kesar flowers provide the *sindūr*
the heroines have given their pride as dowry
Vidyāpati says that Kāma is unfolding this drama.

लता तरुअर मण्डप जीति, निरमल ससधर धबलिए भीति।
पउँअ नाल अइपन भल भेल, रात परीहन पल्लव देल।
देखह माइ हे मन चित लाय, बसन्त बिबाहा कानन–थलि आय।
मधुकर रमनी मंगल गाब, दुजबर कोकिल मंत्र पढ़ाब।
करु मकरंद हथोदक नीर, बिधु बरिआती धीर समीर।
कनअ किसुक मुति तोरन तूल, लाबा बिथरल बेलिक फूल।
केसर कुसुम करु सिंदुर दान, जओतुक पाओल मानिन मान।
खेलए कौतुक नब पँजबान, विद्यापति कबि दृढ कए भान।

10. Beloved

When my beloved returns home
I will make my body the means of ritual to welcome him.
First, I will place my breasts as sacred golden pots,
then looking in the mirror I shall apply *kājala* to my eyes.
My bosom will become the sacred pulpit and
I will spread my hair to sweep it.
I shall position my heavy hips as plantain trees and
the resounding waistband will function as mango leaves.
I will also invite lovely ladies from my neighbourhood,
it will look like a show of many moons spread all over.
Vidyāpati says – your wish will surely be fulfilled,
you are going to meet your beloved within a couple of minutes.

पिआ जब आओब ई मझु गेहे।
मंगल जतहु करब निज देहे।
कनअ कुम्भ करि कुच जुग राखि।
दरपन धरब काजर देइ आँखि।
बेदि बनाओब हम अपन अंक मे।
झाड़ करब ताहे चिकुर बिछीने।
कदलि रोपब हम गरुअ नितम्ब।
आम पल्लब ताहे किंकन सुझम्प।
दिसि दिसि आनब कामिनि ठाट।
चौदिस पसारब चाँदक हाट।
विद्यापति कहे पूरब आस।
दुइ एक पलक मिलब तुअ पास।

1. The Lonesome Lover

Artist: Devemndra Sharma, Chaurapanchashikha style

2. A Bed of Flowers

Artist: Nathulal Verma, Chaurapanchashikha style

3. Śuklābhisārikā

Artist: Kanhaiyalal Verma, Jaipur style

4. Mirror

Artist: Vijay Sharma, Basohli style

5. Master of Love

Artist: Parikshit Sharma, Kangra style

6. Dawn

Artist: Jai Shankar Sharma, Kishangarh style

7. Spring

Artist: Girdhar Khinchi, late Mughal style

8. Time of Love

Artist: Kailash Chand Sharma, Jain style

9. Spring, the Season of Love

Artist: Vijay Sharma, style of Manaku, Guler

10. Beloved

Artist: Kanhaiyalal Verma, Jaipur style